GOD'S
JUDGEMENT
UPON
MANKIND
ABOUT
RAPE

BOOK 1

To order additional copies of this book, contact:
Xlibris
1-888-795-4274
www.Xlibris.com
Orders@Xlibris.com

ISBN: Softcover   978-1-7960-5121-6
          EBook   978-1-7960-5120-9

Print information available on the last page

Rev. date: 08/06/2019

For Lo rape must come to an end for there remaineth no more Salvation for rapist that continue to rape.

For the Lord would speak unto the rapist if they continue on there remaineth no more Salvation.

So I would speak unto the rapist if you continue on in rape you will be condemned.

For the Lord would speak unto thee that the he has heard the cry of women.

For the Lord would also speak unto thee that thou Art saved if thou repent, but if you do not repent you are damned.

For the spirit of Prophecy is the Lord Jesus Christ.

For the Lord again would speak again to the rapist if you do not repent you are condemned.

For the Lord again would speak unto the rapist that if you do not repent you are condemned.

For the Lord again would speak unto the rapist that if you do not repent you are condemned.

For the Lord again would speak unto the rapist that if you do not repent you are condemned.

For the Lord again would speak unto the rapist that if you do not repent you are condemned.

For the Lord again would speak unto the rapist that if you do not repent you are condemned.

For the Lord again would speak unto the rapist that thou Art no forgiveness if you do not repent.

For the spirit of Prophecy is the Lord Jesus Christ.

For the spirit of prophecy is the Lord Jesus Christ.

For the spirit of prophecy is the Lord Jesus Christ.

For the spirit of prophecy is the Lord Jesus Christ.

For the spirit of prophecy is the Lord Jesus Christ.

For the spirit of prophecy is the Lord Jesus Christ.

For the spirit of prophecy is the Lord Jesus Christ.

For the spirit of prophecy is the Lord Jesus Christ.

For the spirit of prophecy is the Lord Jesus Christ.

For the spirit of prophecy is the Lord Jesus Christ.

For the spirit of prophecy is the Lord Jesus Christ.

For the spirit of prophecy is the Lord Jesus Christ.

For the spirit of prophecy is the Lord Jesus Christ.

For the spirit of prophecy is the Lord Jesus Christ.

For the spirit of prophecy is the Lord Jesus Christ.

For the spirit of prophecy is the Lord Jesus Christ.

For the Lord would speak unto thee so therefore be good rapist for I have sinned to sexually after rape happens there's nothing you can do but to forgive yourself but I would say unto thee repent for God demands repentance for there's no way out thou must repent.

For the Lord would say unto thee perish not because of rape, but I would say unto thee again perish not because of rape.

For the Lord would speak unto thee be not afraid of rapist be bold and ask for Angels to surround thee and protect thee and thou shalt be protected by them.

The Martial arts is not very effective against rapist.

But the Lord would speak unto thee that thou shalt not rape women because God almighty is getting tired of it.

But God would speak unto thee get out of rape before you destroy yourself, but the Lord would speak unto thee that rape is a horrible thing for a women to go thru, but my God can deliver thee from rape, so be willing men, but my God is willing to deliver thee, so therefore be delivered men by the Lord Jesus Christ so the Lord would speak unto thee, but my God will supply your every need to get out of rape, men don't worry about rape if you have committed it God will forgive, For God will forgive, For God will forgive.

For the Lord would speak unto thee if you commit rape for the Lord God is able to deliver thee.

For I would speak unto thee that my God is able to deliver thee, the spirit of Prophecy is the Lord Jesus Christ.

For the Lord is worthy to be praised.

For the Lord would speak unto thee that thou art forgiven.

Printed in the United States
By Bookmasters